STEM
Through the Months

Back-To-School Edition
With Student Journals

by

Gary Carnow ■ Beverly Ellman ■ Joyce Koff

For information about Inventive Thinkers® and Clever Thinkers workshops write to:

Inventive Thinkers®
www.inventivethinkers.org
gary@inventivethinkers.org

Clever Thinkers
cleverthinkers@gmail.com

Some illustrations by Sian Bowman and Sandy Stevens

ISBN-13: 978-1511818209
ISBN-10: 1511818204

WELCOME

Welcome to *STEM Through the Months – Back to School Edition, for Budding Scientists, Engineers, Mathematicians, Makers and Poets.* Designed for teachers and students, these activities help you make and create wonderful classroom experiences. Using monthly themed events as a springboard, poetry as a language arts component and the maker movement for inspiration, your students will build cross-curricular connections as they explore STEM – science, technology, engineering and mathematics.

THIS BACK TO SCHOOL EDITION IS DESIGNED FOR YOU

This edition was designed for teachers, students and parents as a companion to the other editions in this series. The activities are primarily for students in grades three through eight. We know you will find these engaging and innovative lessons and projects easy to adopt and adapt for learners of all ages. For each special or silly day in August there is a STEM learning prompt. Need a lesson idea? Simply turn to the day of your choice and your off and running. The projects and poetry lessons have been classroom-tested and provide enjoyable learning experiences in a variety of environments: a traditional classroom, home schooling, after-school programs, scouting, gifted and talented programs, extracurricular clubs and ESL classes. For families looking for weekend or rainy day activities, we think you will find this to be a useful resource. And for kids who thumb through the special days and holidays, we ask, what will you make?

WHAT'S INSIDE?

Inside you will find STEM lessons, projects and poetry experiences inspired by holidays, special days, traditional observances and wacky celebrations. Drawing on the inner poet in every child and the "let me do-it-myself" nature inherent in all learners, the activities and lessons will help your students earn an "A" for the Arts and will bring STEAM to your STEM initiatives. Your budding scientists, mathematicians and engineers will practice creative and inventive thinking skills as they build knowledge throughout the year. Do not feel obliged to use these ideas and projects only in August. The projects and activities are great with their calendar collaborations, but your curriculum and schedule may vary. We encourage you to use the activities and projects on a day that fits into your classroom plans.

HOW IS THIS EDITION ORGANIZED?

We explore the monthly, weekly and movable holidays in August. Whether it's a silly celebration or a traditional holiday, you will find it listed here, ready to kick start the imaginations of your students. Next, Make and Do Days for STEM Learners, Makers and Poets highlight each holiday of the Back to School season with background information and STEM activity starters. Featured are four units of study (science, technology, engineering and math) that coincide with special days and holidays for August. Each major lesson is followed by a poetry lesson that correlates with the unit of study. Students write poems in the style of the selected poet and learn about the poet in a biography that is easily duplicated along with the poem for use in your classroom. Additional poems that enhance the unit are also included. New in this edition are STEM/STEAM journals and booklets.

Correlations to the technology standards from the International Society for Technology in Education (ISTE) and to the Next Generation Science Standards (NGSS) in engineering and science, are included.

STEM/STEAM JOURNALS

Get your students ready for a year of STEM/STEAM activities enriched with student observations and writing. This edition includes hands-on STEM/STEAM journal pages. The pages can be used separately or stapled together. These materials help the inventive thinkers in your classroom:

- state problems
- brainstorm ideas
- choose solutions
- create plans
- construct models or prototypes
- test solutions
- redesign
- evaluate

The hands-on investigations in your classroom will be supplemented by the process standards embedded in the STEM journal pages. Using the journal pages, students practice design thinking as they mess around with the task and materials selected. Students use the journal pages to write in a way that makes sense to them.

Your students will have the choice of generic journal covers or specific covers tied to the science and engineering projects. There is also a generic STEM journal cover and STEAM journal cover for technology and math activities. Following, are small booklet templates to use with all STEM/STEAM lessons. There are booklet templates for poetry, science, technology, engineering and mathematics. These single pages fold into a four-page booklet that your student authors write and embellish with art.

ABOUT STEM

STEM is an acronym for four disciplines: science, technology, engineering and mathematics. These four disciplines are related and overlap, but we tend not to think of STEM as unique unto itself. STEM has become "the next big thing" due to concerns that U.S. students are falling behind and will not be able to fill the void left by an aging workforce. As we become increasingly global dependent, we want our students to be on a level playing field. Educators and parents have no doubt heard the STEM acronym, but are often confused as to what it means or what it actually looks like.

As classrooms adopt STEM activities, teachers and students quickly realize that mathematics is at the core of all STEM disciplines. To be college and career ready, a firm foundation of mathematics is required. Science is also essential and is a part of modern life. Science includes a body of knowledge and the ability to follow methods and processes to construct understanding. There are many scientific disciplines taught in school (for example, life science, earth science, physical science) and they spiral and overlap. Important to the disciplines of science, engineers use scientific thinking to solve problems. K-12 engineering education has long been overlooked. The practical applications of engineering in conjunction with science and math foundations are a necessity. Technology is a part of our everyday life and should be a part of daily school practice. Technology, particularly computing technology, be it handheld devices or desktop computers is a tool that enhances learning. Technology can be an underlying support in all aspects of schooling, not just a tool for STEM disciplines.

As STEM education is adopted in the Common Core State Standards for mathematics and included in the Next Generation Science Standards (NGSS), schools are looking for innovative ways to integrate these highly engaging disciplines. We believe that STEM experiences are important for all students at all grade levels. We see STEM as more than just "real world" – we see it as high engagement and we know that you will find the projects and activities in this book helpful.

STEM GAINS AN "A" – STEAM

The national movement to provide STEM experiences for students gains steam on a daily basis. This is why we have focused heavily on the arts to integrate a big "A" into STEM. We know that you and your students will especially love the core poetry lessons. Students enjoy poetry and learning about famous poets and their poems integrate easily with your STEM and common core focus. From our teaching experience, we have learned that some teachers are uncomfortable teaching poetry. You will be amazed how easily these classroom-tested activities will assist young poets in discovering the joy of writing.

CONNECTION BETWEEN POETRY AND STEM

STEM learning and teaching encourages students to observe their world through their senses. Students construct knowledge through observation and practice in science, technology, engineering and math. This is also true for poetry. By exposure to poets, their lives and their works, students extend their observational skills as they write their own poems. And both poetry and mathematics contain patterns, rhythms and beats. Both are mysterious and need to be understood to comprehend. Then their secrets unfold.

WHY POETRY IS IMPORTANT

Reading poetry out loud reveals a unique rhythm of sounds and beats and, in this way, poetry is immersive and experiential. Students are drawn instinctively to poetry because it allows them the freedom to use language in new and original ways. Students particularly enjoy straying from traditional grammar, capitalization and punctuation in some of their original works. Students are also intrigued by poetry that has an original visual look.

HOW STEM THROUGH THE MONTHS INCORPORATES POETRY

August includes the work of four famous poets. Each selected poet is presented along with a biography, a sample poem and a teaching guide. Most of the poems we have selected are in the public domain. Those that are not are easily found. Your students will call upon their inner voices as they experience writing a poem in the style of the poet that they are studying. Students will also gain an appreciation for the life circumstances and the period of time in which the poet lived and worked. Each poet is matched with a corresponding activity for each facet of STEM (science, technology, engineering and mathematics). The poets are the glue that binds each unit of study in the book and provide a unique language arts underpinning to STEM education.

TECHNOLOGY

We hope that you have access to some classroom or school technology. As technology using educators, we know that it enriches the classroom experience. For over thirty years, students and teachers have used technology tools to add exciting dimensions and high interest to classroom work. We have specifically designed these activities and projects to be enriched through the use of technology; however, it is not a pre-requisite. Paper, pencils and other common classroom supplies will suffice. If you have access to a few computers and a printer, great; we believe strongly in using what you have. There is no need to go out and buy the latest and greatest.

Many schools have employed Chromebooks for use in their classrooms. With a Chromebook, students use Google Docs, Sheets and Slides as their productivity applications. Students create their documents and presentations and store them in the cloud using Google Drive. Students can invite others to collaborate on their documents giving them the ability to edit, view and comment. You can also view a document's revision history and go back to previous versions. Google Docs plays well with Microsoft Word, OpenOffice, Pages and other word processing programs. Similarly, Google Sheets imports and converts from Excel and other spreadsheet file formats, including Numbers. Google Slides shares formats with PowerPoint and Keynote.

Many of the projects in this book use word processing, spreadsheet and presentation software. Whether you have access to computers with that software on the drive or Chromebooks with the application in the cloud, you are set to go. For classrooms with laptops or desktop computers with a hard drive, you have the additional functionality of editing video and using music software. Many tablets and iPads with apps like iMovie and Garage Band will also give you this functionality.

CLASSROOM PUBLISHING

STEM activities and projects come to life through the study and practice of language arts. The International Council of Teachers of English has identified five strands of language arts – reading, writing, speaking, listening and viewing (visual literacy). Students use language arts to show others their thinking, compositions and creativity. Making work "public" validates the work. As early as the one-room schoolhouse, teachers have displayed student writing and drawings. Work was sent home and no doubt "published" on refrigerator doors in the 1930s.

With appropriate technology your students can discover, invent and explore as they publish, illustrate and arrange their written work. These *STEM Through The Months* projects and lessons will be enhanced if you have access to word processing software or classroom publishing software. Your students will enrich their STEM content as they also develop skills in page layout, illustrations, color and typography. Students will also receive value from seeing their ideas "in print," whether they are working on a report or a classroom newsletter. We encourage you to explore the use of a simple digital handheld device, for example, a camera or a tablet, so that students can publish their work to digital lockers, websites or social media.

"STEM'ING" ACROSS THE CURRICULUM

You may be familiar with writing across the curriculum. Today we challenge you to use "STEM'ing" across the curriculum. The activities in this book follow monthly, weekly and daily celebrations across the academic spectrum, including English language arts, mathematics, science, social studies, fine arts, performing arts, and health. STEM learners work in a student-centered learning environment. Their participation is continuously encouraged through questioning, problem solving, collaboration and hands-on activities. Teacher facilitators guide students as they plan and design projects and work in groups to apply the rigors of science, technology, engineering and mathematics contents to achieve their goals.

COMPUTER PROGRAMMING

Now more than ever, schools are looking at ways to add programming into their curriculum. The tools to do so are readily available and even young children are learning to code. Most of the readily available block programming languages are related to Seymour Papert's Logo. Logo is more than just a programming language, it is also a philosophy of education. Logo employs discovery learning and is linked with constructivism, a learning theory. Constructivism relies on students experimenting and solving real-world problems. Students construct their knowledge and understanding through experiences and reflective thought.

A good place to get started is with Scratch, designed for kids at the MIT Media Lab. Scratch is browser-based and is on the web. There are millions of projects created and ready for you to explore, remix and customize to your liking. There are plenty of tutorials and educator websites for you to explore. Get started here at https://scratch.mit.edu/. Scratch works well with many of the projects in this book. In the Mother's Day unit, students make Scratch flowers. As you become familiar with Scratch, presentations and animations can be enhanced. Another similar program to enjoy is Turtle Art. Students can work with powerful mathematical concepts and create beautiful works of art. Get started at turtleart.org.

WHAT IS THE MAKER MOVEMENT?

The maker movement is a revolutionary global collaboration of people learning to solve problems with modern tools and technology. Children and adults are combining new technologies and timeless craft traditions to create exciting projects. The Maker and DIY (Do-It-Yourself) movements are fostering a new enthusiasm to work with your hands and see tangible results. In the 1990s, as we prepared a new generation of "knowledge workers," the goal was to round up all warm bodies and send them off to college, then to a cubicle in a career to fuel the information economy. This vision has not materialized. Now, more than ever, we need people who know how to do things – build houses, fix cars and solve problems.

As the Maker Movement continues to grow exponentially in local communities, makers in on-line spaces and physical spaces are coming together in meet-ups and hackerspaces to create, collaborate and share resources. Makerspaces are popping up in classrooms, libraries and storefronts. These spaces come in many shapes and sizes. A makerspace is not necessarily defined by what tools are contained in the space, but is perhaps better defined by what happens in the space – making.

MAKER TOOLS AND RESOURCES

Many of the lessons and projects in this book can be enhanced with maker tools and resources. The units and lesson extensions are starting points that can be enhanced with some of the exciting maker products now available. There are a variety of these low cost products that work with a computer and will challenge your students. A few to explore include:

- MaKey Makey – http://www.makeymakey.com/
  MaKey MaKey is an invention kit. You turn everyday objects into touchpads and combine them with the Internet. The kit comes with an interface board, alligator clips, a USB cable and instructions. You can use any material that will conduct a bit of electricity to send your computer a keyboard or mouse input. Kids can become artists, engineers and designers as they create projects. They can devise games, mazes, musical instruments and much more.

- Makedo – https://mymakedo.com/
  Makedo are tools for cardboard construction. If you can dream it, you can build it. Makedo are simple plastic parts, a safe-saw, plastic "scrus" and straps that become joints or hinges. Using recycled cardboard you can build anything. Your projects will promote collaboration and problem solving.

- Hummingbird Robotics Kit – www.humingbirdkit.com
  The Hummingbird Robotics Kit enables robotic and engineering activities. It is aimed at ages 13 and up, but works well with ages 8 and up with adult supervision. The kit parts along with crafting materials can make robots, animatronics and kinetic sculptures. Hummingbirds play well with Scratch and other programming languages.

These are just a few of the many creative, open-ended products that your students can use to enhance your curriculum. There is a growing list of materials and kits chock full of creative projects to try. Do a Google search for maker materials and supplies and you will find a wealth of choices. A few examples include Make Magazine (www.makezine.com) and their online store MakerShed; the online store Adafruit (www.adafruit.com); Lego Robotics (http://www.lego.com/en-us/mindstorms/?domainredir=mindstorms.lego.com); and littleBits (http://littlebits.cc/).

3D PRINTING

In this book there are many projects where you could incorporate a 3D printer and use the products you make in some of the activities. Besides the obvious technology and engineering aspects of 3D printing, students can design and prototype projects in a way they could have never done before. Kids have made musical instruments, jewelry and scale models of buildings and monuments and so much more.

As home hobbyists have enthusiastically used 3D printers to make and create a variety of prototypes and products, now your students can, too. The cost of 3D printing has dramatically decreased and schools are beginning to purchase and use 3D printers. There are a variety of printers available and more are being introduced each year. Make magazine has reviews of these printers. Currently, printers for schools and for home use cost from $500 to $2500.

Kids are using computer-aided design programs to create files in the needed stereolithography file format known as .stl. These files are loaded into a 3D printer from your computer. The software that comes with the printer slice these files into layers. The printer begins the additive process of printing an object, layer by layer.

There are many websites where you can get 3D .stl files. Some of these sites feature open source files, which let you modify and customize the files to your liking. You can get an idea of what is available by visiting sites like YouMagine (www.youmagine.com) and Thingiverse (www.thingiverse.com).

NOW LET'S GET STARTED

We think you will find the lessons and projects wonderful additions to your curriculum. We know that *STEM Through the Months for Budding Scientists, Engineers, Mathematicians, Makers and Poets, Back to School Edition* will jumpstart you to make, do and enjoy the school year.

National Ride the Wind Day Lessons and Projects
Poetry Lesson: *The Wind* by Amy Lowell
Science Lesson: Measuring Wind
Wind surfing, kite flying, sailboat racing and just feeling the warmth of the breeze running through your hair are a few of August's delights. National Ride the Wind Day is celebrated on the 23rd of the month. Summer may be coming to an end, but enjoy the warm summer wind and commemorate the first human powered aircraft able to control and sustain its flight.

National Back-to-School Month Lessons and Projects
Poetry Lesson: *The Village Schoolmaster*
by Oliver Goldsmith
Technology Lesson: Famous Former Teachers
Now that summer vacation will soon be a memory, thoughts of school days and our great teachers past, present and future are foremost in our minds. It's time to reflect and look ahead as we enter the new academic year.

National Friendship Week Lessons and Projects
Poetry Lesson: *Inviting a Friend to Supper*
by Ben Jonson
Engineering Lesson: Building a Toy Puppet Theater
National Friendship Week is celebrated August 18th through August 24th. This is a time to appreciate your great friends. Here are a few suggestions to celebrate your friends: send a special home-made greeting card; invite them over for a special day; plan a fun time together; or call just to say hi.

National Sandwich Month Lessons and Projects
Poetry Lesson: *Recipe for a Hippo Sandwich*
by Shel Silverstein
Math Lesson: Sandwich Shop
The name and popularity of the sandwich began in a town known as Sandwich in the County of Kent, England. The Earl of Sandwich loved to gamble and wanted to be able to eat with one hand and gamble with the other. He asked for bread, meat and cheese. Because he needed a hand free for his cards, he put the meat and cheese between two slices of bread. People became aware of the sandwich and it became a popular way of easy eating.

August Monthly Holidays

Children's Vision and Learning Month • Foot Health Month • Harvest Month • International Air Travel Month • National Back to School Month • National Catfish Month • National Golf Month • National Inventor's Month • National Parks Month • National Water Quality Month

August Weekly Holidays

First Week of August
American Soap Box Derby (Akron, Ohio) • Beauty Queen Week (1st-7th) • International Clown Week • National Smile Week • Simplify Your Life Week • Turtles International Awareness Week

Second Week of August
Diving Week • Don't Wait – Celebrate Week • Elvis Week • International Festival Week • National Apple Week • National Recreational Scuba Week

Third Week of August
Air Conditioning Appreciation Week • American Dance Week • Freedom of Enterprise Week • National Aviation Week • National Hot Lava Week • Weird Contest Week

Last Week of August
Be Kind to Humankind Week • Carpenter Ant Awareness Week

August Moveable Holidays

Sister's Day...first Sunday

Nut Monday...first Monday

National Night Out ....first Tuesday

Family Day .... second Sunday

Hopi Snake Dance...third Saturday

August Days for STEM Makers and Poets

Day		Make and Do
1	The first U.S. Census in 1790	*There are lies, damned lies and statistics.* - *Mark Twain* When the first census was taken in 1790, 3,939,326 citizens were counted in 16 states and the Ohio Territory. That number is 12% of today's population. Have your students work in groups to discover five key facts about your hometown or your state. Get ready to integrate your Math lessons with graphs, statistics and maps.
2	Friendship Day	Friendship Day was the brainchild of Joyce Hall, the founder of Hallmark. August 2nd was selected as there were no major August holidays. Makers will enjoy creating friendship bracelets. Poets, pick up your pencils and begin with: "Friendship is." Engineers, create your own musical greeting card, by searching "how to make a musical greeting card?" Artists, explore Tapigami with your best friend.
3	National Watermelon Day	Watermelons are refreshing because they are 92% water. Europeans introduced them to America. Research, gather and make a watermelon cookbook. How will you enjoy them, sliced, diced or grilled? Be sure to include history of the watermelon. If your school has a community garden, try your hand at planting a county fair winning melon.
4	United States Coast Guard Day	Coast Guard families celebrate the day with a picnic. Learn about the illustrious history of the United States Coast Guard at http://www.uscg.mil/history/. Listen to and research "Semper Paratus (Always Ready)" the official marching song written by Captain Van Boskerck.
5	American Bandstand	American Bandstand (AB) broadcast on national television on this day in 1957. Hosted by Dick Clark, it brought rock 'n' roll music, dance steps, and fashion to millions of teenagers. Watch some AB clips and create your own "Rate-A-Record" segment.
6	Lucille Ball Day	Lucille Ball was born on August 6, 1911. In the 1950s, she and her bandleader husband Desi Arnaz, created the popular I Love Lucy Show. Virtually visit the Lucy-Desi Museum at <www.lucy-desi.com>. Full episodes as well as her famous Vitametavegamin segment can be seen at: <http://www.cbs.com/shows/i_love_lucy/>. Why not make your own Vitameatavegamin commercial?

7	National Lighthouse Day	This day commemorates the great historical significance of the lighthouse. Although its use has declined due to the arrival of radar and GPS technology, the lighthouse remains a symbol of safety and security for boats at sea. Research and build a replica of a lighthouse with common household items and a working light at top.
8	Happiness Happens Day	Today is the day to be happy, spread the joy and look on the brighter side of life. Play Pharrell William's Happy song, dance around the room and create your own happy music video.
9	Moment of Silence for Nagasaki, Japan	On August 9, 1945 at 11:02 a.m., the atomic bomb was dropped on Nagasaki, Japan. On this day and time people around the world observe a moment of silence to honor those who lost their lives to the A-bomb. This brought an end to World War II and saw the beginning of the nuclear age. Search the Internet to learn about the use of nuclear power. Debate the positive and negative effects of its use.
10	The Smithsonian Institution is Established in 1846	The Smithsonian Institution is a group of nineteen museums, nine research centers and a zoo in Washington, D.C. Design your own classroom museum. Make museum exhibits displaying topics that you are studying. For example, how about a museum of technology innovations?
11	Play in the Sand Day	Today is all about building sandcastles, digging holes and of course enjoying the ocean. Learn how at: http://www.theguardian.com/lifeandstyle/2009/aug/01/how-to-build-perfect-sandcastle.
12	Vinyl Record Day	Today is the day Thomas Edison invented the phonograph in 1877. How are vinyl records made and how do they work? Find a few albums and head on down to the malt shop and spin some tunes. Design an album cover of your favorite record.
13	International Lefthanders Day	Celebrate your right to be left-handed. Make a list of the advantages and disadvantages of being left-handed.
14	National Creamsicle Day	Popsicles were invented by an 11 year old boy in 1905. Two billion are sold each year including Creamsicles. Invent your own Creamsicle by combining your favorite ice cream and popsicle flavors using paper cups and popsicle sticks and freezing them.
15	National Relaxation Day	Some interesting poems are lists. Wind down, breathe easy and relax on this special day. Make a list of all things that are relaxing to you and turn them into a list poem.
16	Elvis Has Left the Building Day	Elvis Aaron Presley was born in a two-room house in Tupelo, Mississippi on January 8, 1935 and died on August 16, 1977. He starred in thirty-three movies. Take a virtual tour of Graceland. Create a virtual tour of where you live.

17	First American Steamboat Trip in 1807	Robert Fulton produced the first commercially successful steamboat. Try your hand at building a toy steamer that runs on heat and the water that it floats on. Make Magazine's Pop-Pop steamboat is ready for you to build at http://makezine.com/projects/make-28/pop-pop-steamboat/.
18	Rotten Rhyme Day	Bad Poetry Day was developed by wellcat.com and is copyrighted. So instead, write some really bad rhymes today and celebrate Rotten Rhyme Day.
19	Ogden Nash Birthday	Frederic Ogden Nash (August 19, 1902 – May 19, 1971) was an American poet well known for his puns and rhymes. Write a poem in the style of Ogden; you will find a collection of his poems at http://www.westegg.com/nash/. His poem *Fleas* goes like this: Adam. Had'em.
20	National Chocolate Pecan Pie Day	Chocolate Pecan Pie recipes began in the mid 1920s. Celebrate this food holiday by learning about Karo syrup and trying out their recipe.
21	Hawaii Statehood Day	Hawaii joined the Union on this day in 1959; the most recent state of the 50 U.S. States. Hawaii is the only state made up of Islands and is the home of active volcanoes. Test out your own Baking Soda Volcano at http://www.weatherwizkids.com/experiments-volcano-baking-soda.htm.
22	Be an Angel Day	Established by Jayne Howard Feldman in 1993, Be An Angel Day is the day to perform a random act of kindness. There are many ways to celebrate - write a poem for a friend, do a good deed, or volunteer your time.
23	Permanent Press Day	Today is the perfect day to learn about the history of irons and ironing. Create your own iron on transfers for t-shirts, napkins, etc. by printing your favorite black and white designs on the waxy side of freezer paper.
24	National Peach Pie Day	This day falls right in the middle of the peach harvest season. Celebrate this delicious fruit by finding an easy to make recipe on the Internet.
25	National Don't Utter a Word Day	This is a day for listening instead of talking. If it is not a school day, give it a try! Write an essay about what you heard on the day you didn't speak.
26	Women's Equality Day Begins in 1974	Women were granted the right to vote on August 20, 1920 with the certification of the 19th Amendment to the United States Constitution. The amendment was first introduced in 1878. How does an amendment to the Constitution pass?
27	Guinness Book of World Records	First published on August 27, 1955, learn all about it at http://www.guinnessworldrecords.com/explore-records/. Create a class record book of students' amazing feats such as jumping the highest, adding a long row of addition problems the quickest, having the longest hair, and so on.

28	Anniversary of the 1963 March on Washington	The anniversary of The March on Washington for Jobs and Freedom, led by Dr. Martin Luther King, took place in Washington, D.C., on August 28, 1963. Today we commemorate "Dream Day." Read the Dream speech and write a paragraph about your future dreams for equality and our country.
29	Chop Suey is invented in New York City in 1896.	Pass the chopsticks and enjoy some chop suey. It may have been invented in New York City in 1986. How and where Chop Suey was really invented is a bit murky so why not create your own story about its origins?
30	National Marshmallow Toasting Day	Using standard ½ inch PVC pipe, pipefittings and a bag of mini marshmallows, build a marshmallow shooter. With just a puff of air you can shoot 40 feet or more. Directions are at the Make Magazine website – makezine.com.
31	National Trail Mix Day	Trail mix is a tasty high-energy treat often made of nuts, dried fruits, seeds and more. Mix equal parts for a delicious treat. Create and name your own mix and design the packaging.

Science Lesson for National Ride the Wind Day: How Do You Measure the Wind?

An anemometer is used to measure the speed of the wind. In this lesson, students work in groups to build and experience how this weather station instrument is used in meteorology and aerodynamics.

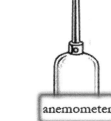

anemometer

MATERIALS
- White board or chart
- For each group of students: five, three-ounce paper cups, two plastic straws, a long straight pin, sharpened pencil with unused eraser, dark-colored permanent marker, tape, scissors, paper and pencils.
- Groups can share small staplers and paper punch

PLAN
- Discuss wind measurement with the class encouraging student input of personal knowledge and experiences.
- An anemometer (after the Greek word anemos meaning wind) is an instrument used to measure wind speed.
- Wind is caused by the difference in pressure that results when air molecules move from higher to lower concentrations (areas of high and low pressure).
- Wind speed measurement is important for:
  1. Weather prediction (meteorology)
  2. Aircraft and maritime operations
  3. Construction
  4. Outdoor sports
  5. Alternative energy placement

DO
- Students build a simple anemometer using spinning paper cups that measure the speed of the wind as they turn.
- Divide class into groups and distribute materials.
- Group members determine how to assemble the anemometer completing the following steps:
  1. Using a hole punch, punch one hole in four of the paper cups about ½ inch below the rim. The cups will catch the wind and cause the anemometer to spin. The more spins per minute, the greater the wind velocity.
  2. In the remaining fifth cup, punch four equally spaced holes ¼ inch below the rim.

3. Make a hole in the center of the bottom of the fifth cup using scissors and a push pin or a hole punch. This hole needs to be large enough for the pencil to go through it.

4. Push a soda straw through the hole of one of the first four cups; fold the end of the straw and either staple or tape it to the side of the cup across from the hole. Repeat this action with a second cup and straw. cups onto the end of the pushed through straw. Bend the straw and staple or tape it to the cup making sure that the cups on both sides face the opposite direction.

5. Repeat the previous direction with the remaining two cups.

6. Next slide the straw through the two remaining one-holed cups onto the end of the pushed through straw. Bend the straw and staple or tape it to the cup making sure that the cups on both sides face the opposite direction with the first cup attached through two opposite holes in the four-hole cup. Attach one of the two remaining one-holed

7. Align the four cups making sure they all face the same direction. This is necessary so that when wind pushes a cup, it turns away from the wind, exposing the next cup to wind from the same direction.

8. Use the marker to color the inside of one cup to make it easier to count the revolutions.

TIME TO EXPERIMENT

- The anemometer rotates with the wind. Students use the completed anemometer to collect their data.
- Count and record the number of times the cup rotates in a minute.
- Determine the number of rotations at various locations.
- How do the number of rotations change from an open playground or between two classrooms?
- The number of rotations give a simplified description of wind speed.
  0-5 rotations .... Calm
  6-29 rotations .... Light
  30–39 rotations .... Moderate
  40–61 rotations .... Strong
  62 or more rotations .... Hurricane
- For older students, calculate the velocity at which the anemometer spins by determining revolutions per minute (RPM). Determine in feet, the circumference made by the rotating paper cups. Calculate velocity in feet per minute by multiplying the RPM by the circumference of the circle.

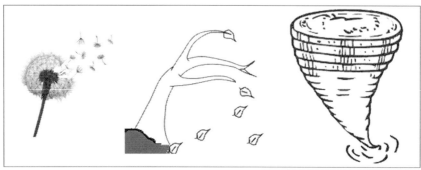

Poetry Lesson for National Ride the Wind Day: The Wind

In her poem *The Wind,* Amy Lowell uses personification as she describes the wind as a friendly and mischievous character who "steals the down from the honeybee." He is a magical character: "Laughing, dancing, sunny wind, /Whistling, howling, rainy wind." The wind is not a force to fear, but loveable with four faces north, south, east and west, all of which the poet likes "the best."

MATERIALS
- Amy Lowell Biography and poem *The Wind*
- Word processing or desktop publishing software or pencils, pens and paper

PLAN
- Read and discuss Amy Lowell's biography and poem.
- Sample guiding questions include:

  - Who is "He?" How does Lowell make you feel about the wind?
  - Where does she use personification?
  - How do the objects touched by the wind feel about him?
  - What does he do to make them feel that way?
  - How many personalities does the wind possess?
  - What interesting verbs and adjectives does Lowell use?

DO
Getting Ready to Write
- Using imagination and experience, students brainstorm a list of things the wind effects.
- Enhance the list using personification as they answer the following questions:
  1. What verbs would you use to express the way the wind speaks?
     For example: *shouts, laughs, wails*
  2. What adjectives would you use to describe the wind's personality?
     For example: *invigorating, energetic, powerful*
  3. How do the objects you're writing about interact with the wind?
     For example: *trees wait to be tickled, the ocean waves its fingers*

Writing the Poem
- Students write a poem about the wind referring to it by using the pronoun he or she.
- Suggest they begin their poem describing how the wind speaks or acts to an object and how the object interacts with the wind.
- Have them continue their poem repeating the previous direction with new objects.

Editing and Publishing
- Have students read and edit poems with partners.
- Students compose or publish their poems in a word processing program.
- Students illustrate their final masterpieces.
- Create a class book or publish to a web site.

Amy Lowell Biography
February 9, 1874 – May 12, 1925

Amy Lowell was born in Brookline, Massachusetts. She was the youngest of five children. Lowell was from one of the most prominent families in New England. An English governess began teaching her to read and write when she was five or six. She was sent to school at age eight. By then she had developed a strong love of reading and had even begun some writing.

Lowell was very heavy from the time she was eight years old. As an adult, at only five feet tall she weighed 240 pounds. Her obesity made her self-conscious; so self-conscious that she didn't like being at school. Lowell loved the theater and may have become an actress if it weren't for her weight. Between the ages of 13 and 15, she wrote poetry. After that time she stopped writing until she was 28 and continued writing until her death. She became the founder of Imagism, a form of poetry which aimed particularly at "image" or clear pictures of what the poet had in mind. Lowell's reading tours helped to make the new poetry a matter of national interest.

At the height of her fame people had to be turned away from the auditoriums and halls she used. Even people who did not admire her poetry acknowledged her power over a live audience. In her final years she achieved her greatest success as a public reader.

From the time she began writing poetry, she felt that poetry had chosen her. After her death, a book containing some of Lowell's best and most mature poems was awarded the Pulitzer Prize.

The Wind
by Amy Lowell

He shouts in the sails of the ships at sea,
He steals the down from the honeybee,
He makes the forest trees rustle and sing,
He twirls my kite till it breaks its string.
Laughing, dancing, sunny wind,
Whistling, howling, rainy wind,
North, South, East and West,
Each is the wind I like the best.
He calls up the fog and hides the hills,
He whirls the wings of the great windmills,
The weathercocks love him and turn to discover
His whereabouts -- but he's gone, the rover!
Laughing, dancing, sunny wind,
Whistling, howling, rainy wind,
North, South, East and West,
Each is the wind I like the best.

The pine trees toss him their cones with glee,
The flowers bend low in courtesy,
Each wave flings up a shower of pearls,
The flag in front of the school unfurls.
Laughing, dancing, sunny wind,
Whistling, howling, rainy wind,
North, South, East and West,
Each is the wind I like the best.

Technology Lesson for National Back-to-School Month: Famous Former Teachers

At the beginning of the school year, students wonder who their teacher will be. Students will be surprised to find out how many famous people have been teachers. In this lesson, students work in pairs and search the Internet for the names of famous people who have been teachers for part of their careers. Students choose a famous person they would have liked to have for a teacher. After gathering information, students write an essay about why they selected this person and the positive and negative traits they think the teacher possessed.

MATERIALS
- Internet-capable device
- Word processing software
- Paper and pencil

PLAN
- Students share teacher traits they do and don't admire.
- Working in pairs, students search the Internet for lists of famous former teachers and review and share their findings with the class.
- Teacher demonstrates and leads students in practice note-taking exercises and reviews how to cite Internet websites.

DO
- Each student selects a former famous teacher as the subject of his/her personal essay.
- Information is gathered from various websites.
- Students write a three-paragraph essay to include background information in the first paragraph; traits they admire and those they could overlook in the second paragraph; and what it might be like to be in that teacher's classroom in the third paragraph.
- Students format their essays and include a picture.
- Files are saved and printed for a classroom book or bulletin board.
- Students recite their essays to the class.

Poetry Lesson for National Back-to-School Month: The Village School Master

Oliver Goldsmith introduces us to an important "village schoolmaster" in his life in the poem *The Village Schoolmaster*. This detailed and honest dedication tells of his teacher's "severe" countenance that "every truant knew" and of his kindness and "love he bore to learning." His schoolmaster may have been forgotten if not for this poem.

MATERIALS
- Oliver Goldsmith Biography and poem *The Village Schoolmaster*
- Word processing or desktop publishing software or pencils, pens, and paper

PLAN
Read and discuss biography and poem. Some sample guiding questions include:
- How does the setting draw us into the poem?
- Why did the schoolmaster frighten some students?
- Why did the students laugh at all their teacher's jokes?
- What were the schoolmaster's virtues?
- Why was the child happy to be taught by a stern teacher?

DO
Getting Ready to Write
- Have students think about and visualize an influential teacher.
- Students close their eyes and visualize the images that come to mind.
- The class discusses their thoughts.
- Encourage students to describe both physical and character details.
- Record descriptions as they are discussed, listing each one on a separate line.
  For example:
  A smile was on her face.
  She stood by the board.
  She smelled like chalk.

Writing the Poem
- Using *The Village Schoolmaster* as a model, students write their own influential teacher poem.
- Begin the first line of the poem by describing the image they see in their mind's eye.
- Students continue writing by including more details.
  For example: appearance, personality, traits, habits and gestures
- Each detail becomes a separate line of their poem.

Editing and Publishing
- Students trade papers with a partner. Each draws the teacher their partner described in his/her poem.
- Students write their poems in a poetry book or enter them in a word processing program.

Oliver Goldsmith Biography
November 10, 1730 – April 4, 1774

Oliver Goldsmith was born in a small village in Ireland. His father was a farmer and the head of a local church. After being educated at home he began school where he was bullied because of his small size and because his face was scarred from smallpox. He was not considered very bright and was mistreated by his teachers. But even at a young age, he showed a talent in writing and also loved reading great literature.

In college he was considered a character because he dressed in bright colors where most people of that time did not. After graduating college, where he was not a good student and where he was always getting into trouble, he traveled through France and Germany and wrote about these travels. He probably earned money for his food and lodging by performing with his flute. He loved music and gambling and was always in debt. With his talent in writing and his need for money, he began working for a publisher where he produced some impressive literary work. He wrote plays and poetry. One play was called "The History of Little Goody Two-Shoes" from where the saying "goody two shoes" probably comes.

Goldsmith wrote the truth that he saw in a sweet and gentle way and most of his writing describes happy memories. In his lifetime he became friends with many famous artistic people not only for his writing but also his kind nature. After his death his friends placed a monument to honor him in Westminster Abbey at the Poet's Corner featuring a bust of his profile. A monument was also erected in his honor in Ireland.

Poetry historians believe it is possible that the village schoolmaster was Goldsmith's teacher when he was six years old.

The Village Schoolmaster
by Oliver Goldsmith

Beside yon straggling fence that skirts the way
With blossom'd furze unprofitably gay,
There, in his noisy mansion, skill'd to rule,
The village master taught his little school;
A man severe he was, and stern to view,
I knew him well, and every truant knew;
Well had the boding tremblers learn'd to trace
The days disasters in his morning face;
Full well they laugh'd with counterfeited glee,
At all his jokes, for many a joke had he:
Full well the busy whisper, circling round,
Convey'd the dismal tidings when he frown'd:
Yet he was kind; or if severe in aught,
The love he bore to learning was in fault.
The village all declar'd how much he knew;
'Twas certain he could write, and cipher too:
Lands he could measure, terms and tides presage,
And e'en the story ran that he could gauge.
In arguing too, the parson own'd his skill,
For e'en though vanquish'd he could argue still;
While words of learned length and thund'ring sound
Amazed the gazing rustics rang'd around;
And still they gaz'd and still the wonder grew,
That one small head could carry all he knew.
But past is all his fame. The very spot
Where many a time he triumph'd is forgot.

Illustrations by members of "The Etching
Club" published in Bolton Corney, ed.,
The Poetical Works of Oliver Goldsmith, Lee
and Shepard, Boston, 1872

Engineering Lesson for National Friendship Week: Building a Toy Puppet Theater

Toy theater kits were popular in the late 18th and early 19th century. Each kit included the stage, scenery, characters and costumes from a popular story. Everything that was needed to put on a puppet play was included in the kit. In this group project, students write friendship plays, design puppets and make a puppet theater. Plays can be performed for classmates, family members and others in the school community.

MATERIALS

- Cardboard boxes about the size of computer or packing boxes, sharp scissors or packing knife, tape, etc. for the stage
- Wallpaper, fabric, ribbon, fancy paper, miniature furniture, art material, plants etc. for scenery
- Craft paper, clothes pins, craft sticks, tongue depressors, string, wire, glue, paint, paper, fabric, paper towel and toilet paper rolls, paper bags, pipe cleaners, yarn, googly eyes, brads, etc. to create the puppets
- Handout – Building a Toy Theater Kit and Writing a Friendship Play

PLAN

- Discuss the popularity of toy theaters in the late 18th and early 19th century. Explain that the original toy theaters, which were printed on paperboard, were sold in kits and included the stage, scenery, and characters from well-known stories or plays. Today makers and crafters create their own toy theaters from scratch. There are many toy theater productions available on YouTube. If possible watch one or two with students.
- Brainstorm story ideas for a toy theater National Friendship Day puppet show. Suggest that students write about friendships from a favorite book such as "Charlotte's Web," actual friendships, and stories from their life or imaginary friendships. List some of their story ideas on the board.
- Place materials available for the puppet shows on a table or workspace for students to use as they create their toy theater kits and produce their plays.
- Distribute and discuss the Directions for Building a Toy Theater handout.

DO

- Divide the class into groups to use provided materials, found materials and their imaginations to create their toy theater kits.
- Each group writes a script for their production describing the characters and dialogue.
- Group members decide on roles for completion of the production including: theater construction; props, music, sound and lights; puppet makers; puppeteers.

Building a Toy Theater Kit and Writing a Friendship Play

The play you write and the puppets you design will determine the kind of Toy Puppet Theater you will create.

WRITING THE FRIENDSHIP PLAY

- Create a story about friendship involving two or more characters. You may wish to model your story from a favorite book.
- Describe your characters and write your script.
- Decide what type of puppets to make. For example, some sample puppets include stick, paper bag, glove, finger, marionettes and cardboard roll.

BUILDING YOUR PUPPETS AND THE TOY PUPPET THEATER

- Select a cardboard box for the theater. The theater you create will depend upon the type of puppets you plan to use. For example, you could create a stage window by cutting an opening in the front of the box. A theater for marionettes will need an opening at the top.
- Find and select materials to use for puppets, sets, scenery and props.

PRODUCING THE PLAY

- Rehearse and practice your play.
- Edit and rewrite as necessary.
- Is there sufficient dialogue to make the story clear?
- Is the stage constructed to allow enough room for the puppeteers to move the puppets freely?
- Are the actors speaking loudly enough for everyone to hear?

Poetry Lesson for National Friendship Week: Inviting a Friend to Supper

Ben Jonson's poem is an invitation to a friend. Johnson invites a friend to supper, enticing him to attend by describing a sumptuous meal. Not only does he bribe his friend with food, he also writes that his friend will be entertained by a reading of Virgil along with several other Roman poets while they dine. This is a perfect poem for Friendship Week where the students will invite a friend of theirs to breakfast, lunch or dinner.

MATERIALS
- Ben Johnson Biography and poem *Inviting a Friend to Supper*
- Word processing or desktop publishing software or pencils, pens and paper, fancy stationery or art materials to create stationery.

PLAN
Read and discuss biography and poem. Some sample guiding questions include:
- What does he promise his friend to convince him to come to supper?
- What does he promise the entertainment to be?
- What does he promise will not be part of the entertainment?
- What does he say to convince his friend that they will be happy the next morning?

DO
Getting Ready to Write
Students discuss the follow questions:
- If you were to invite your friend to a meal, which meal would it be?
- What qualities does your friend have that makes you want to invite him or her?
- What would you promise your friend to insure that he or she will come?
- How would you exaggerate the occasion to make it so great that there is no way he or she would turn it down?
- What would you say to make your friend know how much you want him or her there?
- How would you let your friend know that coming would make him or her happy tomorrow?

Writing the Poem
- Suggest students write a poem in which they invite a friend to a meal.
- Begin poems with "Please come to my home [whenever]"
- Continue the poem with the words "my friend" and describe something about their friend that makes him or her the person they want to invite.
- Describe what they will be served in an exaggerated and extraordinary way.
- End with how they will feel after such a great event.

Editing and Publishing
- Students embellish their poem with a fancy border and print.
- Students exchange printed invitations to find out if the person reading their invitation would be enticed to join them.

Ben Jonson Biography
June 11, 1572 – August 8, 1637

Ben Jonson was born June 11, 1572. Shortly after his father's death, when he was one month old, his mother remarried. His stepfather was a bricklayer and for a while Jonson worked in this trade as well. He escaped from his work by joining the army. When he returned to London he met the woman who was to be his wife, Anne Lewis.

Jonson loved the theatre, not only did he write dramas but also acted in them. He was imprisoned for writing and acting in a play that poked fun at the queen and government officials. Not long after that he killed a fellow actor in a duel. He was once again imprisoned. He escaped the gallows narrowly and when released from prison he was left penniless. Jonson continued to write plays that incited the law and was imprisoned repeatedly. He was impatient and known for having a temper. He thought of himself superior to most people because of his talent.

Jonson wrote plays called "masques" for the entertainment of the court. In these plays he demonstrated his great wit and wrote some of his best poetry. He was appointed Court Poet. He then wrote a series of comedies that were considered his best work, and was named poet laureate.

When he grew old he was supported by the king and kept comfortable by his friends who never left him. Jonson was honored by being buried at Westminster Abbey. In many peoples' opinion he was, next to William Shakespeare, the greatest dramatic genius of his time.

Inviting a Friend to Supper
by Ben Johnson

Tonight, grave sir, both my poor house, and I
Do equally desire your company;
Not that we think us worthy such a guest,
But that your worth will dignify our feast
With those that come, whose grace may make that seem
Something, which else could hope for no esteem.
It is the fair acceptance, sir, creates
The entertainment perfect, not the cates.
Yet shall you have, to rectify your palate,
An olive, capers, or some better salad
Ushering the mutton; with a short-legged hen,
If we can get her, full of eggs, and then
Lemons, and wine for sauce; to these a cony
Is not to be despaired of, for our money;
And, though fowl now be scarce, yet there are clerks,
The sky not falling, think we may have larks.
I'll tell you of more, and lie, so you will come:
Of partridge, pheasant, woodcock, of which some
May yet be there, and godwit, if we can;
Knat, rail, and ruff too. Howsoe'er, my man
Shall read a piece of Virgil, Tacitus,
Livy, or of some better book to us,
Of which we'll speak our minds, amidst our meat;
And I'll profess no verses to repeat.
To this, if ought appear which I not know of,
That will the pastry, not my paper, show of.
Digestive cheese and fruit there sure will be;
But that which most doth take my Muse and me,
Is a pure cup of rich Canary wine,
Which is the Mermaid's now, but shall be mine;
Of which had Horace, or Anacreon tasted,
Their lives, as so their lines, till now had lasted.
Tobacco, nectar, or the Thespian spring,
Are all but Luther's beer to this I sing.
Of this we will sup free, but moderately,
And we will have no Pooley, or Parrot by,
Nor shall our cups make any guilty men;
But, at our parting we will be as when
We innocently met. No simple word
That shall be uttered at our mirthful board,
Shall make us sad next morning or affright
The liberty that we'll enjoy tonight.

Math Lesson for National Sandwich Month: Sandwich Shop

In this group project, students become both diners and restaurateurs as they create a special Sandwich Shop Menu for National Sandwich Month. Once all menus have been created, groups will exchange menus and become diners. They will need to order at least five items from the menu. Depending on their math level they can do some or all of the following: add the bill, compute the tax and tip, and divide the bill between the group members to see how much each should pay.

MATERIALS

- Smart board or chart
- Internet access and word processing software (optional)
- Card stock paper
- Paper and pencils
- Art supplies, crayons, paints, colored pencils, markers, etc.

PLAN
- Students brainstorm to create a list of favorite restaurant sandwiches.
- After student responses are captured, ask students to give brief descriptions of their favorite sandwich. Jot a few notes next to the various selections.
- Students will work in groups to create a special Sandwich Shop menu. Students name their Sandwich Shop, create a menu and open for business. The menu should have five sections (appetizers, main course, sides, beverages and desserts). All items in the main course section are special sandwiches with illustrative descriptions. The prices should range from $1.00 to $15.00 per item.

DO
- Divide class into four or five groups.
- Group members plan their menus by creating, describing and pricing items for the five sections of their menu. Encourage students to include their own restaurant favorites.
- They write the menu selections, descriptions and prices on a "professionally designed" menu with the Sandwich Shop's name at the top. The final product is created using card stock paper and art supplies or if available they can create their menu on a word processor and add graphics from the Internet.
- Groups exchange menus and become diners using each other's menus.
- Each "diner" orders a meal of at least three items from the menu and totals up his/her bill.
- Depending on the math ability of the group, students add tax and tip to their meal. The group can total all the diner's meals and divide to split the bill equally between all diners at the table.
- The Sandwich Shop menu can be displayed on a bulletin board celebrating National Sandwich Month.

Poetry Lesson for National Sandwich Month: Recipe for a Hippopotamus Sandwich

In this delightful poem, Shel Silverstein, in his imaginative and original way, writes a recipe for a hippo sandwich. This is a perfect poem for National Sandwich Month where children will imagine and write a poem about their own unusual sandwich and discover the challenges in devouring their creation.

MATERIALS
- Shel Silverstein's biography and summary of his poem
- Word processing or desktop publishing software or pencils, pencils, pens and paper

PLAN
Read and discuss the biography and poem. Some suggested questions include:
- What ingredients in the recipe are found in the home or market?
- What ingredients work together in most sandwiches?
- What are the ingredients besides the hippopotamus that are not usually in a sandwich?
- What is the most unusual and silly ingredient?
- What might be the challenge in eating this sandwich?

DO
Getting Ready to Write
Have students brainstorm the following questions:
- What kind of sandwich will you write about?
- What usual and unusual ingredients will be in your sandwich?
- What would it be like to eat your sandwich?

Writing the Poem
- Students write a poem in which they make an unusual sandwich.
- Suggest they begin their poem with "A (name of sandwich) is easy to make"
- Have them continue their poem interspersing usual and unusual ingredients they will use.
- Have them write the most unusual and silliest ingredient last.
- End the poem with revealing something challenging about taking your first bite.

Editing and Publishing
- Have students check for errors with a partner.
- Students may wish to share their poems in a poetry book.
- Students illustrate their poem with Shel Silverstein style cartoons of their sandwich.

Shel Silverstein Biography
September 25, 1930 - May 10, 1999

Shel Silverstein was born in Chicago, Illinois. He was a talented and diversified artist. Silverstein was a popular poet and prose writer for young readers. He was also a well-known cartoonist, recording artist and songwriter. As a songwriter he won a Grammy and was nominated for an Oscar.

He lived his early years with his parents, Nathan and Helen Silverstein. As a child, he was not popular since "When I was a kid—12 to 14, around there—I would much rather have been a good baseball player or a hit with the girls, but I couldn't play ball. I couldn't dance. Luckily, the girls didn't want me. Not much I could do about that. So I started to draw and to write."

Silverstein attended Roosevelt High School in Chicago. After his graduation he began studying art at the Chicago Academy of Fine Arts now known as Art Institute of Chicago. He loved music and studied for a short time in a college for the performing arts.

He dropped out of college, joined the Army and had his cartoons published in the *Pacific Stars and Stripes* magazine. The editions were delivered to the troops on the front line so they could get the latest news. The soldiers enjoyed his drawings.

Silverstein was best known for his poetry. He also created the illustrations in his books. Two of his most popular books are *Where the Sidewalk Ends*, and *A Light in the Attic*. In all of his poetry, his readers are carried away by his unique imagination and his way of playing with words. Both the young and old throughout the world have been captured by his silly and serious poems.

Recipe for a Hippopotamus Sandwich
from Where the Sidewalk Ends by Shel Silverstein

In his poem, Shel Silverstein begins in a simple way letting the reader know about how easy it is to make a hippopotamus sandwich. He begins his recipe with ingredients that are found in most kitchens although not usually combined in one sandwich such as bread, some cake and an onion ring. The poem ends as he discovers a problem with the sandwich when he adds the final ingredient, a hippo.

The entire poem is available online. You can search for it by typing the words "Recipe for a Hippopotamus Sandwich" by Shel Silverstein or you can go to the following website and find the poem. It is ready to print, copy, and share with your class.

http://allpoetry.com/poem/8538979-Recipe-For-A-Hippopotamus-wbr--Sandwich-by-Shel-Silverstein

For a small fee, you can purchase a movie of the poem "Recipe for a Hippopotamus Sandwich" from iTunes. The poem is recited along with illustrations of all the ingredients that are necessary for this sandwich.

You can also find the movie on YouTube.
https://www.youtube.com/watch?v=hdi-FPWwk60

Additional Back-to-School Poems
by William Blake, John Greenleaf Whittier and Walt Whitman

The School Boy by William Blake
November 28, 1757 – August 12, 1827

I love to rise in a summer morn
When the birds sing on every tree;
The distant huntsman winds his horn,
And the sky-lark sings with me.
O! what sweet company.

But to go to school in a summer morn,
O! it drives all joy away;
Under a cruel eye outworn,
The little ones spend the day,
In sighing and dismay.

Ah! then at times I drooping sit,
And spend many an anxious hour,
Nor in my book can I take delight,
Nor sit in learnings bower,
Worn thro' with the dreary shower.

How can the bird that is born for joy
Sit in a cage and sing?
How can a child when fears annoy,
But droop his tender wing,
And forget his youthful spring?

O! father & mother, if buds are nip'd
And blossoms blown away,
And if the tender plants are strip'd
Of their joy in the springing day,
By sorrow and care's dismay.

How shall the summer arise in joy,
Or the summer fruits appear?
Or how shall we gather what griefs destroy,
Or bless the mellowing year,
When the blasts of winter appear?

from In School-Days by John Greenleaf Whittier
December 17, 1807 – September 7, 1892

Still sits the school-house by the road,
A ragged beggar sleeping;
Around it still the sumachs grow,
And blackberry-vines are creeping.
Within, the master's desk is seen,
Deep-scarred by raps official;
The warping floor, the battered seats,
   The jack-knife's carved initial;
The charcoal frescoes on its wall;
Its door's worn sill, betraying
The feet that, creeping slow to school,
Went storming out to playing!
Long years ago a winter sun
Shone over it at setting;
Lit up its western window-panes,
And low eaves' icy fretting.
It touched the tangled golden curls,
And brown eyes full of grieving,
Of one who still her steps delayed
When all the school were leaving.
For near it stood the little boy
Her childish favor singled;
His cap pulled low upon a face
Where pride and shame were mingled.
Pushing with restless feet the snow
To right and left, he lingered;---
As restlessly her tiny hands
The blue-checked apron fingered.
He saw her lift her eyes; he felt
The soft hand's light caressing,
And heard the tremble of her voice,
As if a fault confessing.
"I'm sorry that I spelt the word:
I hate to go above you,
Because,"---the brown eyes lower fell,---
"Because, you see, I love you!"

from An Old Man's Thought of School by Walt Whitman
May 31, 1819 – March 26, 1892

For the Inauguration of a Public School, Camden, New Jersey, 1874

An old man gathering youthful memories and blooms that youth itself cannot.
Now only do I know you,
O fair auroral skies--O morning dew upon the grass!
And these I see, these sparkling eyes,
These stores of mystic meaning, these young lives,
Building, equipping like a fleet of ships, immortal ships,
Soon to sail out over the measureless seas,
On the soul's voyage.
Only a lot of boys and girls?
Only the tiresome spelling, writing, ciphering classes?
Only a public school?
And you America,
Cast you the real reckoning for your present?
The lights and shadows of your future, good or evil?
To girlhood, boyhood look, the teacher and the school.

Extension Lesson: Thinking Skills –
A Multiple Choice Test About Our Teacher

In this lesson, students will hone their interviewing skills and learn about their teacher as they conduct and post teacher interviews. The information students gather will be used to create a multiple choice test about their teacher to see how much they have learned.

MATERIALS
- Pencil and paper
- Tag paper and markers or cut bulletin board letters

PLAN
During a class discussion in the first month of school, tell the students they are going to create questions for a multiple-choice test about you. Begin the project with the class brainstorming a list of information they want to learn about you. Help them create a list that is varied and includes feelings, likes, dislikes, personal information etc. Some sample questions could be:
- What is your favorite food?
- Where were you born?
- Do you have any pets?
- What famous person would you like to meet?
- How many people are in your family?
- What makes you laugh?
- If you could trade lives with a famous person who would you choose?
- Where did you go on your last vacation?

DO
- Have students fold a paper in half lengthways. On the left-hand side have them write five questions they want to know about you, skipping a few lines after each questions. During the week have them come up to you at appropriate times that you designate and get the answers to their questions. Have them write their answers in the right-hand side.
- Title a bulletin board All About <Your Name> and have students put the completed question/answer sheets on the board. This is a perfect bulletin board to leave up for Back-to-School Night to introduce yourself to the parents.
- Encourage the students to read the board during their free time telling them you are going to create a multiple choice test using their questions and answers when the board is complete.
- Create and distribute the test. Once the test is completed go over the questions and answers with the students.

Extension Lesson:
An Old Man's Thought of School by Walt Whitman

Walt Whitman wrote about what school was like when he was young in the poem
An Old Man's Thought of School. In this lesson, students explore what an older adult in
their family thinks about school when he or she was young.

MATERIALS
Paper, pencils, pens

PLAN
After reading the poem, *An Old Man's Thought of School,* have students interview the oldest
person they can interview in the next few days.

DO
- Have them ask the person to tell them what they think about when they are remembering
  his/her school days.
- During the interview students write down the older person's memories and
  what they have learned.
- Have them identify the person and if possible give the person's age.
- Students share their interviews with the whole class.

STEM BACK-TO-SCHOOL LEARNING STANDARDS
For Budding Scientists, Engineers, Mathematicians, Makers and Poets

NGSS Standards and Learning Objectives	
3-5 ETS1-1 Define a simple design problem reflecting a need or want that includes specified criteria for success and constrains on materials, time, or cost.	Given the challenge of designing and building a theater for a toy puppet show with found materials, students will define the challenge and specify the criteria for a successful performance.
3-5 ETS1-2 Generate and compare multiple possible solutions to a problem based on how well each is likely to meet the criteria and constraints of the problem.	Students will generate multiple solutions to design puppets. They will evaluate the various possibilities to decide which to use, for example stick, paper bag, glove, finger, marionettes and cardboard roll.
4-PS3-4 Apply scientific ideas to design, test, and refine a device that converts energy from one form to another.	Students will design a device (anemometer) to measure wind speed in order to use the wind's energy to create movement of objects.
4-ESS3-1 Obtain and combine information to describe that energy and fuels are derived from natural resources and their uses affect the environment..	Students will calculate the wind speed using an anemometer to observe the potential effect the wind's energy can have on the environment.
NCTM Standards and Learning Objectives	
5.NBT Perform operations with multi-digit whole numbers and with decimals to 100s.	Students will work with multi-digit whole numbers with decimals to 100's as they price and calculate menu items.
4.OA Use the four operations with whole numbers to solve problems.	After creating and exchanging menus, students will use whole number operations to order food, total their bills, compute the tax and tip, and divide the cost per person.
ISTE Standards and Learning Objectives	
4.6 Conceptualize, guide and manage individual or group-learning projects using digital planning tools with teacher support.	Students are able to work in groups and in pairs using digital note taking tools to create a strategy for developing and completing a project.
7 Select and use appropriate tools and digital resources to accomplish a variety of tasks and to solve problems.	Students are able to select the appropriate tools (drawing programs, Internet, word processors, etc. to create and present personal essays.
NCTE/IRA Standards	
3 Students a wide range of strategies to comprehend, interpret and evaluate text.	Students will apply a wide range of strategies to comprehend, interpret, appreciate and write poetry.

STEM Journal

Engineering Journal

Building a Toy Puppet Theater

Science Journal

Measure the Wind

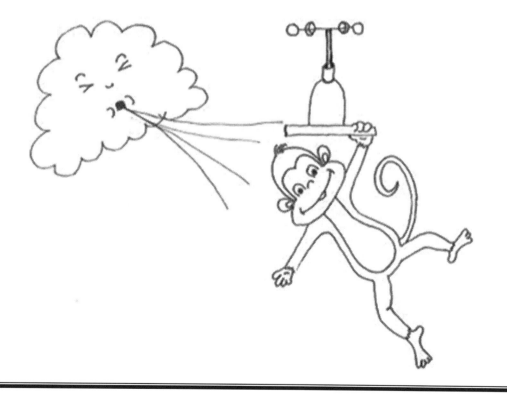

State The Problem

_____

_____

_____

List the Requirements

_____

_____

_____

_____

_____

_____

_____

_____

_____

_____

_____

_____

_____

Brainstorm Ideas

- ★ _____
- ★ _____
- ★ _____
- ★ _____
- ★ _____
- ★ _____
- ★ _____
- ★ _____
- ★ _____
- ★ _____
- ★ _____
- ★ _____
- ★ _____
- ★ _____
- ★ _____
- ★ _____
- ★ _____
- ★ _____
- ★ _____

Choose a Solution

Why this solution?

What materials will you use?

Create a Plan

Explain your plan.

_____

_____

_____

_____

Draw a diagram.

Construct a Model

Write a description and/or draw an illustration of the finished model in the space below.

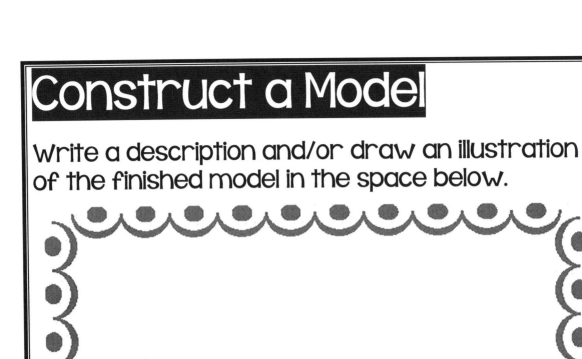

Test Your Solution

Does it meet your requirements?
Describe any problems.

Redesign

Improve your solution.

_____

_____

_____

_____

_____

_____

Conclusion

What have you learned?

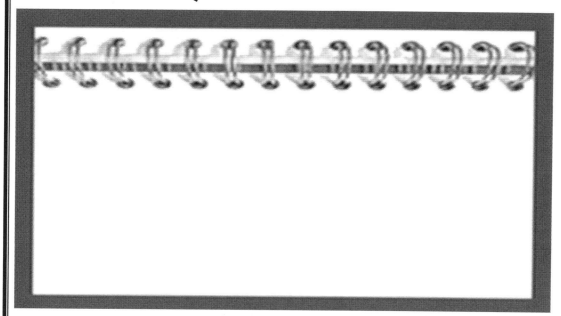

How can you use what you have learned in the future?

Technology Journal

Technology Project

Project Name_____

Describe the end product. Begin with the end in mind.

_____

_____

_____

_____

_____

Make a plan. What steps will you take?

1. _____

2. _____

3. _____

4. _____

5. _____

Technology Resources

Hardware

_____ _____

_____ _____

_____ _____

Software

_____ _____

_____ _____

_____ _____

Websites

_____ _____

_____ _____

_____ _____

Self Reflection

*We do not learn from experience ...
we learn from reflecting on experience.*
– John Dewey

What did you learn?
What were the key strengths of your project?
What would you change next time?

_____

_____

_____

_____

_____

_____

_____

_____

_____

_____

Tech Tools and Apps

<u>Art, Graphics and Photo Software</u>
Corel Paint Shop
Kid Pix Deluxe 4 and Kid Pix 3D
Photoshop and Photoshop Elements
Tux Paint (free)

<u>Education Suites</u>
Adobe Creative Cloud (monthly subscription)
Apple Keynote, Numbers, and pages (bundled with a Mac)
Google Apps (Classroom, Gmail, Drive, Calendar, Docs, Sheets, Slides, and Sites)
Microsoft Office Suite
Open Office (free)

<u>Interactive Applications</u>
HyperStudio
ThingLink

<u>Miscellaneous Apps</u>
Chartgo (free)
Create A Graph (free)
Comic Life
GarageBand (bundled with a Mac)
Inspiration, Kidspiration and Kidspiration Maps (lite version free)
Timeliner

<u>Presentation</u>
PowToon (basic version free)
Prezi (free trial available)

<u>Programming/Coding</u>
Scratch (free)
Tynker (free version available, subscription plans too)
Hopscotch (free)

<u>Search Engines</u>
Duck Duck Go (free)
Google and Google Kiddle (free)

<u>Video Editing</u>
Adobe Premiere Elements
Adobe Premiere Pro (subscription)
Animoto (free trial available)
WeVideo (web based, free trial available)
iMovie (free with Mac purchase)
Loopster (web based, basic version free)
WeVideo (web based, free trial available)

Poetry
Journal

Biography

Name of poem _____

Name of poet _____

When did the poet live? _____

What did you learn about the poet?

_____

_____

_____

_____

_____

_____

_____

_____

Brainstorming

Words: What interesting and/or descriptive words are in the poem?

★ _____
★ _____
★ _____
★ _____
★ _____
★ _____
★ _____
★ _____
★ _____
★ _____

Phrases: Cite the figurative language (like similes personification, and metaphors) that you found in the poem.

★ _____
★ _____
★ _____
★ _____
★ _____
★ _____
★ _____
★ _____
★ _____

Writing Your Poem

Write the first line of the poem you read.

_____

_____

Write the first line of your poem using the poet's first line as a model.

_____

_____

Refer to your brainstormed word and phrase list as you continue to write your poem.

_____

_____

_____

_____

_____

_____

_____

_____

_____

_____

_____

Illustrating Your Poem

Create an illustration for your poem.

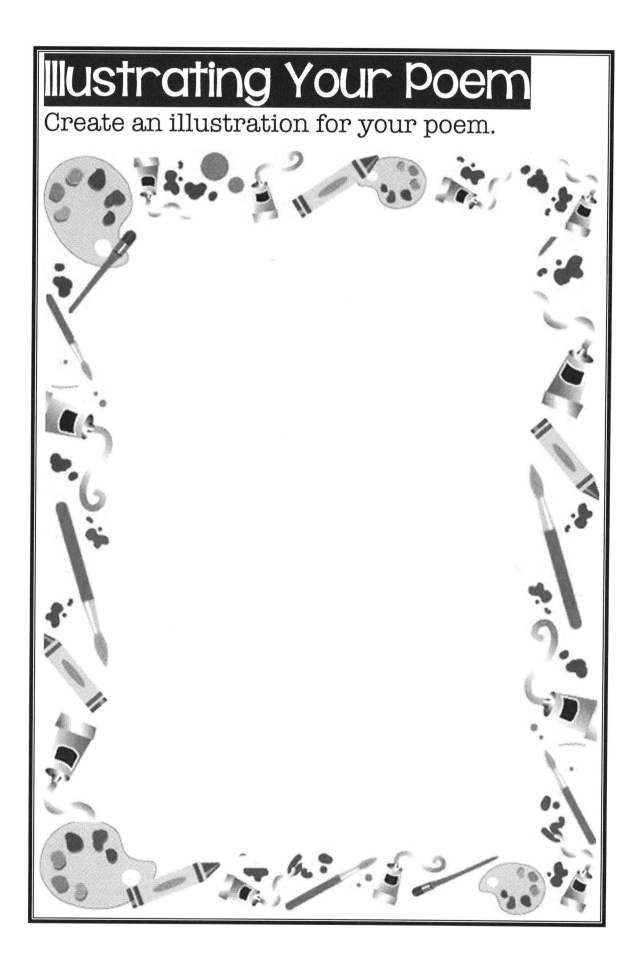

Math Journal

Solving Math Problems

Date _____

Select a math problem from this week's lessons.
State the problem and the solution.

Problem	Solution

Math Process

Explain how you solved the problem.

_____

_____

List and define any math vocabulary or terms that you used.

Math Word	Definition

What skills did you use?

_____

_____

What facts did you need to know?

_____

_____

How do these skills apply to real world problems?

_____

_____

_____

_____

Extend Understanding

Illustrate the problem by drawing one of the following: picture, chart, graph, table, diagram, model or symbol in the space below.

What tools and/or digital devices would help? Why?

_____

_____

_____

_____

Reflections

How do you feel about your performance on the math concepts we learned this week?

_____

_____

_____

Which did you find the most interesting?

_____

_____

_____

Which need further practice?

_____

_____

_____

How does this week's work affect the way you feel about math?

_____

_____

_____

SCIENCE JOURNAL

State the Problem

2

Choose a Solution

3

4

TECHNOLOGY JOURNAL

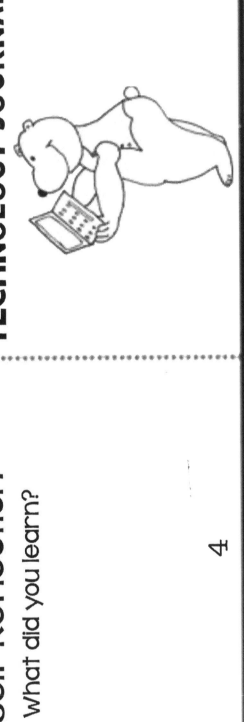

Technology Project

Project Name _____

Describe your project.

What steps will you take?

2

Technology Resources

3

Self Reflection

What did you learn?

4

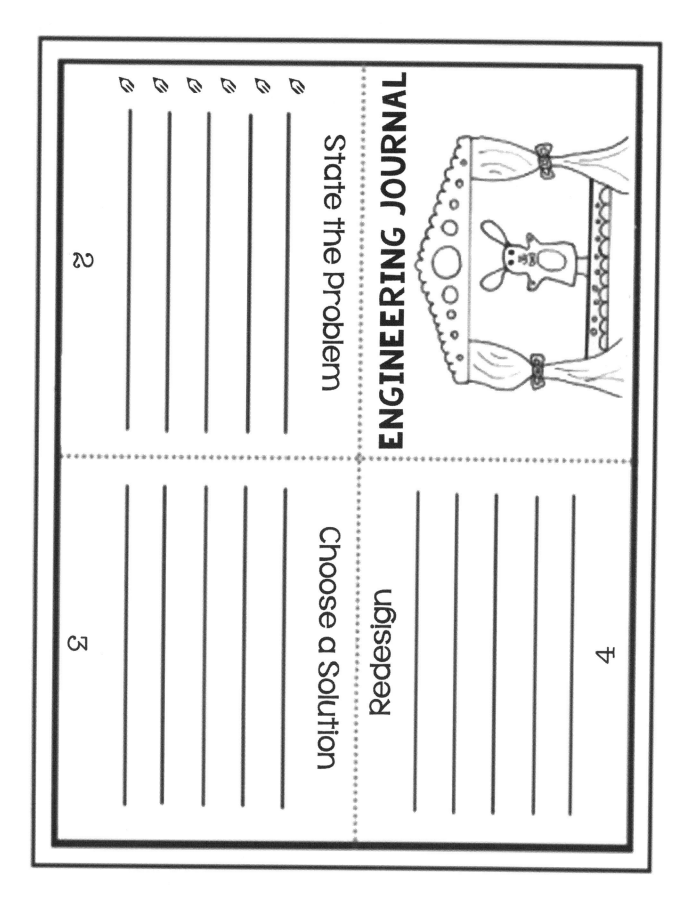

ENGINEERING JOURNAL

State the Problem

2

Choose a Solution

3

Redesign

4

POETRY JOURNAL

Biography

Name of Poem _____

Name of Poet _____

What did you learn about the poet?

2

Brainstorming

What interesting, descriptive and/or figurative language can you find in the poem?

3

Writing

Refer to the brainstormed list as you write your poem.

4

MATH JOURNAL

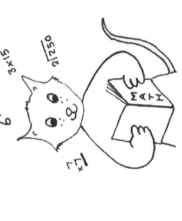

$9, 6$
3×15
$2\overline{)250}$
$\mathrm{M A T H}$

Math Process

Explain how you solved the problem.

What skills did you use?

2

Solving Math Problems

Select a math problem from this week's lessons. State the problem and the solution.

Problem	Solution

3

Extending Undestanding

Illustrate the problem by drawing one of the following: picture, chart, graph, table, diagram, model or symbol in the space below

4

About Us

GARY CARNOW has been a classroom teacher, administrator, author and educational consultant. Dr. Carnow specializes in administrative and instructional technologies, grants and funding procurement, instructional program development, emerging technologies, makerspaces and 3D printing. He has consulted for major hardware and software computer companies and has written extensively for Tech&Learning magazine. He was one of the first educators to provide content for AOL and the Scholastic Network. Beverly and Gary have written educational materials together for over twenty-five years.

BEVERLY ELLMAN is an educator who has enjoyed wearing many different hats. She has been a classroom teacher, an author of educational publications and an educational product developer. She has co-taught several classes which combined poetry and multimedia through UCLA extension with Joyce Koff. In addition, Joyce and Beverly have worked together presenting educational workshops to various elementary and middle school teachers. She has enjoyed watching the enthusiasm, energy, and creativity sparked in students as they experience learning and master STEM content.

JOYCE KOFF is a poet and a teacher. Her work has been published in numerous poetry journals and she has taught in elementary and middle schools in her self-created program. Joyce makes the reading, understanding and writing of poetry accessible to all students and these methods are applied in this book. Joyce has also conducted classes at UCLA demonstrating to teachers how valuable and rewarding the teaching of hands-on poetry can be. As the resident poet at Coeur d'Alene Elementary School in Venice, California, she taught poetry for over 25 years and was part of the art's team that was awarded the prestigious Los Angeles Music Center's Bravo Award.

SIAN BOWMAN has never lost the giddy excitement she experienced as child when drawing and painting. After graduating from Aberystwyth University with a Masters in Fine Art, specializing in children's book illustration, she started freelancing as an illustrator. She is in her element working on picture books and educational books for children. She finds inspiration for her characters in walking her wonderful, cheeky whippet, Jet, through the countryside of Mid Wales - where her imagination can wander. You can learn more about Sian at sianbowman.com.

SANDY STEVENS has a diverse background as an educator, musician and artist. Her 35 years in education were spent as a classroom teacher, counselor , and principal. During her tenure in education, she used art and design as a way to communicate and engage students and colleagues. She enjoys bringing a smile to her audience with her drawings. Sandy can be contacted at sketchbandit51@gmail.com.

Made in the USA
San Bernardino, CA
12 July 2016